For _____

Dedicated to _____

Date _____

The Hats that Laura and Murray Wear!

ISBN: 978-0-578-35859-8

Copyright © 2022 by Kim Lewis

All rights reserved.

Illustrated by Alvin Cadiz

Design and Layout by BelieversBookServices.com

No part of this book may be reproduced, transmitted, or stored in an information retrieval system in any form or by any means, graphic, electronic, or mechanical, including photocopying, taping, and recording, without prior permission in writing from the publisher.

Printed in the United States of America

First Edition 2022

For more information about this book or its authors, please contact: Kim Lewis at kimlewishomes@gmail.com

The Hats that Laura and Murray Wear!

Kim Lewis

Illustrated by Alvin Cadiz

This book is dedicated to my sweet son, Carter Reed, who I was blessed with after nine years of praying.

Laura and Murray are next-door neighbors and often play together after school.

They love to wear hats and make believe.

"Look at this hat!" says Murray. "It's in the shape of a ball cap but it's too small for my head & feels hard. When I wear it, I have to walk very carefully or it will fall off my head."

"That's really a funny looking hat!" says Laura.

Laura puts on a crown.
"That's not a hat!" says Murray.

"Yeah, but I feel really beautiful when I have it on," Laura says. "Like I'm a princess!"

Murray takes the hard cap off his head and puts on a bowl instead.

"Why do you have a bowl on your head?" says Laura.

"To see how long it will stay on," Murray replies. His mom calls him inside, and he walks to her with the bowl staying put on top of his head.

"Bye, Laura!"
"Bye, Murray!"

The next day comes and Laura stands in her driveway waiting to play.

"Murray!" she calls. "Look what I have for you! It's a fireman's hat! We learned about fire safety at school today. What did you learn about?"

"I learned about safety, too," Murray says as he puts on the fireman hat. He walks over and grabs a cup of water that he just finished drinking from & puts it on Laura's head.

"I don't get it…" she says. "The cup is for when you need water to put out a fire!" Murray says.

"Good idea!" she agrees.

"Watch out, Murray! There's a huge hole in the ground!" Laura says.

"Oh, no!" Murray springs into action. "Let me grab my construction hat and shovel."

Murray ends up overfilling the hole, and now there is a huge pile of dirt on the ground. Laura pats it into rounded mound.

"This looks like a mountain!" Laura says.

"Yeah, I have a mountain in my yard!" The kids laugh. "I'm going to grab my cowboy hat and ride my pony around the mountain."

Laura's mom calls her in for supper.

"Bye, Murray!"
"Bye, Laura!"

A couple days pass, and the weekend arrives. It's actually Murray's birthday celebration, and he wants everyone to wear a hat.

It's a hat-themed birthday party!

Bobby wears a Pirate hat. Sarah wears a tall red-and-white striped top hat. Laura wears a sequined unicorn hat, and Murray wears a train conductor hat.

"I love to put on a hat and pretend I'm a superhero and somewhere magical. It's so exciting!" Murray says.

Murray's mom chimes in and says, "Don't forget that it's good to be you, too... the magical person that each of you are!"

Kim Lewis is the author of *The Hats that Laura and Murray Wear!*

A realtor & property manager by day, novelist by night, she received her Bachelor of Business degree from Bellevue University and is a veteran of the USAF.

A Kansas native, she is a lover of fitness, nachos, and mountains but most importantly her family. This book is dedicated to her sweet son, Carter Reed, who she was blessed with after nine years of praying.

www.ingramcontent.com/pod-product-compliance
Lightning Source LLC
Chambersburg PA
CBHW061403160426
42811CB00100B/1443